TODAY YOU CHANGED the WORLD

written by
MAGGIE HUTCHINGS

illustrated by
EVIE BARROW

affirm press

Today the world changed.

It wasn't on the radio

but today

in a town like yours

Indie wasn't allowed to play.

She asked

Why?

Today
Indie changed minds
and discovered

she was brave.

You might not know about this

but today

in a schoolyard

Billy heard a child cry.
He held their hand
when no-one else would.

Today
Billy healed their heart
and said

I'll stand with you.

It never made the newspapers
but today
in a war zone

Mia read about a library
with no books.

She said
This must change!

Today
Mia made change happen
and learnt

she was strong.

It wasn't on the internet
but today
on a street like mine

Bella gave her lunch
to a boy with no home.

Today
Bella showed kindness
and a seed of hope grew

in the soul of a stranger.

No-one said anything to you
but today
on a mountain top

Li saw a falling star and
wrote a poem for everyone.

Today
Li wrote words of beauty
and shared them

with the world.

It wasn't on TV
but today
on our planet

children sang songs of change

and acted with great kindness.

Tomorrow
a million small things
will make a big difference.

Tomorrow

you'll change the world.

Today you already did.